THE UlTIMATE GUIDE TO CBT: Transform Your Life with Proven Strategies for Overcoming Depression, Anxiety, Insomnia, Intrusive Thoughts, and Anger.

DONALD E. STANFIELD

About the Author

Donald E. Stanfield is a licensed therapist and a renowned expert in the field of Cognitive Behavioral Therapy (CBT). With over 20 years of experience in the mental health field, he has helped countless individuals overcome their mental health challenges and achieve greater well-being.

Donald's passion for CBT stems from his deep understanding of its effectiveness in treating a wide range of mental health issues. Through his work, he has witnessed firsthand the transformative power of CBT and is a source for anyone looking to improve their mental health and well-being.

Chapter 1:

Understanding Cognitive Behavioral Therapy (CBT)

What is CBT?

Mental Conduct Treatment (CBT) is a broadly utilized and proof-together psychotherapy approach that concentrates on the connection between contemplations, sentiments, and ways of behaving. It depends on the possibility that our contemplations and convictions impact our feelings and activities and that by changing our considerations and ways of behaving, we can change how we feel. CBT is a cooperative and objectively situated treatment that normally includes an organized and time-restricted treatment plan. It centers around distinguishing and changing pessimistic ideas examples and ways of behaving that add to close-to-home trouble. CBT advisors work with clients to foster survival techniques and critical thinking abilities to deal with their side effects and further develop their general prosperity.

The History of CBT

CBT was created during the 1960s by specialist Aaron T. Beck, who at first utilized it to treat sorrow. After some time, CBT has developed and extended to address an extensive variety of psychological wellness issues, including uneasiness problems, fears, dietary problems, and substance misuse. The advancement of CBT was impacted by before types of psychotherapy, like conduct treatment and mental treatment. Conduct treatment zeroed in on changing maladaptive ways of behaving through methods like openness treatment and support, while mental treatment zeroed in on distinguishing and testing negative ideas examples, and convictions.

How CBT Works

CBT depends on the mental model, which recommends that our considerations and convictions impact our feelings and behavior. As per this model, pessimistic and silly considerations can prompt close-to-home pain and maladaptive ways of behaving. CBT advisors work with clients to distinguish and challenge these negative ideas examples and convictions, and to foster more versatile perspectives and acting. CBT is a cooperative and objective situated treatment that commonly includes an organized and time-restricted treatment plan. It centers around recognizing and changing pessimistic ideas examples and ways of behaving that add to close-to-home trouble. CBT advisors work with clients to foster survival techniques and critical thinking abilities to deal with their side effects and further develop their general prosperity.

The Core Principles of CBT

The center standards of CBT include:

- **Mental Rebuilding:** Recognizing and testing negative and nonsensical contemplations and convictions.
- **Social Enactment:** Expanding commitment in sure and compensating exercises to develop mindset further and diminish side effects of sadness.
- **Openness Treatment:** Progressively presenting clients with dreaded circumstances or upgrades to decrease nervousness and fears.
- **4 Critical thinking:** Creating successful critical thinking abilities to address life stressors and difficulties.
- **Schoolwork Tasks:** Empower clients to rehearse new abilities and systems beyond treatment meetings.

The Benefits of CBT

CBT have been broadly explored and have been demonstrated to be compelling in treating an extensive variety of psychological wellness issues. A portion of the advantages of CBT include:

- The time has come restricted and zeroed in on unambiguous objectives, making it a practical treatment choice.
- It is exceptionally organized and can be adjusted to meet the singular requirements of clients.
- It shows clients pragmatic abilities and techniques that they can use to deal with their side effects and further develop their general prosperity.
- It has been demonstrated to be pretty much as powerful as medicine in treating sadness and uneasiness problems, and it might make longer-enduring impacts.

In outline, CBT is an exceptionally viable and proof put together treatment approach that concentrates on changing pessimistic ideas examples, and ways of behaving to work on profound prosperity. It is a cooperative and objective situated treatment that shows viable abilities and procedures that clients can use to deal with their side effects and work on their general personal satisfaction.

Chapter 2:

The Cognitive Component of CBT

Understanding Cognitive Distortions

Mental twists, otherwise called thinking blunders or mental inclinations, are nonsensical and pessimistic idea designs that can add to close-to-home pain and maladaptive ways of behaving. Normal mental twists include:

1. **Win big or bust Thinking:** Seeing things in high contrast terms, disregarding the ill-defined situations or subtleties.

2. **Overgeneralization:** Making expansive and clearing decisions given a solitary occasion or piece of proof.

3. **Catastrophizing:** Expecting the absolute worst result will occur, regardless of whether there is no proof to help it.

4. **Personalization:** Getting a sense of ownership with things that are unchangeable as

far as you might be concerned or faulting yourself for things that are not your issue.

5. **Mind Perusing:** Expecting you can read others' minds or feelings with practically no proof to help it.

Identifying and Challenging Negative Thoughts

This is a vital part of CBT. This includes becoming mindful of your viewpoints and convictions and scrutinizing their precision and legitimacy. A few inquiries you can pose to yourself to challenge negative contemplations include:

- Is there any proof to help this idea?
- What might I tell a companion who had this thought?
- Is there a more adjusted or reasonable method for pondering this circumstance?
- What might occur on the off chance that I didn't trust this idea?

Cognitive Restructuring Techniques

Cognitive rebuilding is a procedure utilized in CBT to help clients distinguish and challenge negative idea designs and supplant them with additional versatile and reasonable considerations. Some normal mental rebuilding strategies include

- **Thought Halting:** Hindering negative contemplations by saying "stop" or imagining a stop sign.
- **Mental Reexamining:** Taking a gander at a circumstance according to an alternate point of view to track down a more sure or adjusted understanding.
- **Decatastrophizing:** Inspecting the proof for and against a horrendous idea to diminish its effect.
- **Socratic Addressing:** Posing yourself a progression of inquiries to challenge the precision and legitimacy of a negative idea.

Thought Records and Cognitive Journaling

Thought records and mental journaling are apparatuses utilized in CBT to assist clients with following their contemplations and distinguishing designs. An idea record is a worksheet that helps clients distinguish and challenge negative considerations. At the same time, mental journaling includes recording negative contemplations and examining them to recognize mental twists and foster more versatile perspectives.

In synopsis, the mental part of CBT centers around recognizing and testing negative idea examples and supplanting them with additional versatile and sensible considerations. This includes figuring out mental bends, distinguishing and testing negative contemplations, utilizing mental rebuilding procedures, and utilizing thought records and mental journaling to follow and dissect considerations.

Chapter 3:

The Behavioral Component of CBT

Behavioral Activation

Social enactment is a critical part of CBT that spotlights expanding commitment in sure and compensating exercises to further develop the mindset and lessen the side effects of misery. It depends on the possibility that a downturn is frequently connected with an absence of inspiration and delight in exercises. By expanding commitment to charming exercises, state of mind can be reached to the next level. Social initiation includes:

- Recognizing and booking agreeable and compensating exercises.
- Defining explicit and attainable objectives for these exercises.
- Checking and following advancement.
- Recognizing and provoking hindrances to commitment in exercises.

Exposure Therapy

Openness treatment is a method utilized in CBT to assist clients with step-by-step defying and defeating fears and fears. It depends on the possibility that aversion to dreaded circumstances or improvements can keep up with tension and forestall adjustment. Openness treatment includes:

- Making a progressive system of dreaded circumstances or upgrades, from least to most nervousness inciting.

Progressively presenting the client to these circumstances or boosts, beginning with the least uneasiness inciting and stirring up to the most nervousness inciting

- Empowering the client to defy their feelings of dread and remain in the circumstance until their uneasiness diminishes.
- Rehashing openness practices until the client no longer encounters uneasiness in the circumstance.

Behavioral Experiments

Social examinations are a method utilized in CBT to assist clients with testing the precision of their convictions and suspicions. It depends on the possibility that convictions and presumptions can be tried through direct insight and that this can prompt more precise and reasonable convictions. Conduct tests include:

- Distinguishing a conviction or presumption that the client needs to test.
- Planning a trial to test the precision of this conviction or suppositio
- Leading the trial and noticing the outcomes.
- Thinking about the outcomes and amending the conviction or presumption if vital.

Activity Scheduling

Action booking is a strategy utilized in CBT to assist clients with expanding commitment to certain compensating exercises. It includes:

- Recognizing and booking explicit exercises that the client appreciates or views as fulfilling.
- Laying out unambiguous and attainable objectives for these exercises.
- Observing and following advancement.
- Distinguishing and provoking boundaries to commitment in exercises.

In rundown, the conduct part of CBT centers around expanding commitment in certain and compensating exercises, going up against and beating fears and fears, testing the exactness of convictions and presumptions through direct insight, and expanding commitment in sure and remunerating exercises. This includes procedures like conduct enactment, openness treatment, social trials, and movement planning.

Chapter 4:

Applying CBT to Depression

Understanding Depression

Discouragement is a typical psychological well-being problem described by steady sensations of misery, sadness, and a deficiency of interest or joy in exercises. It can likewise be joined by actual side effects like changes in craving or rest, exhaustion, and trouble concentrating. Wretchedness can fundamentally affect an individual's satisfaction and work, and it is vital to look for treatment if you are encountering side effects of melancholy.

CBT Techniques for Depression

CBT is a viable treatment for melancholy, and there are a few methods that can be utilized to assist with overseeing side effects. A portion of these methods include:

- **Mental Rebuilding:** Recognizing and testing negative idea examples and supplanting them with additional versatile and reasonable considerations.
- **Social Enactment:** Expanding commitment in certain compensating exercises to develop mindset further and lessen side effects of wretchedness.
- **Movement Planning:** Recognizing and booking explicit exercises that the client appreciates or views as fulfilling.
- **Thought Records:** Following and breaking down bad considerations to recognize mental contortions and foster more versatile perspectives.
- **Unwinding Strategies:** Learning and rehearsing unwinding procedures like profound breathing, moderate muscle unwinding, and directed symbolism to diminish pressure and nervousness.

Contextual investigations and Examples

Contextual investigations and models can assist with showing how CBT methods can be applied to gloom. For instance, a contextual investigation could portray a client who is encountering side effects of sorrow, like low mindset, weakness, and trouble concentrating. The advisor could utilize mental rebuilding to help the client distinguish and challenge negative idea designs, for example, "I'm useless" or "Nothing at any point goes appropriate for me." The specialist could likewise involve social enactment to assist the client with expanding commitment in sure and compensating exercises, like investing energy with companions or chasing after leisure activities. After some time, the client could see a decrease in side effects and an improvement in their general prosperity.

In synopsis, CBT is a successful treatment for sadness, and there are a few methods that can be utilized to assist with overseeing side effects. These strategies incorporate mental rebuilding, conduct enactment, action planning, thought records, and unwinding procedures. Contextual analyses and models can assist with outlining how these procedures can be applied to wretchedness and can give trust and motivation to the individuals who are battling with this condition.

Chapter 5:

Applying CBT to Anxiety

Understanding Anxiety

Uneasiness is a typical psychological well-being problem described by inordinate concern, dread, and worry. It can likewise be joined by actual side effects like quick heartbeat, perspiring, and shaking. Uneasiness can fundamentally affect an individual's personal satisfaction and work, and it is essential to look for treatment on the off chance that you are encountering side effects of nervousness.

CBT Procedures for Anxiety

CBT is a powerful treatment for tension, and there are a few procedures that can be utilized to assist with overseeing side effects. A portion of these methods includes:

- **Mental Rebuilding:** Distinguishing and testing negative idea examples and supplanting them with additional versatile and practical contemplations.
- **Openness Treatment:** Step by step presenting the client to dreaded circumstances or boosts to decrease tension and fears.
- **Unwinding Strategies:** Learning and rehearsing unwinding methods like profound breathing, moderate muscle unwinding, and directed symbolism to decrease pressure and tension.
- **Care:** Rehearsing care strategies, for example, contemplation and care-based pressure decrease to expand mindfulness and acknowledgment of considerations and feelings.

Contextual Analyses and Examples

Contextual analyses and models can assist with delineating how CBT procedures can be applied to nervousness. For instance, a contextual investigation could portray a client who is encountering side effects of tension, like unnecessary concern and a feeling of dread toward social circumstances. The specialist could utilize mental rebuilding to help the client recognize and challenge negative idea designs, for example, "I'm not adequate" or "Everybody is deciding for me." The specialist could likewise utilize openness treatment to help the client step by step face and defeat their anxiety toward social circumstances. Over the long haul, the client could see a decrease in side effects and an improvement in their general prosperity.

In outline, CBT is a viable treatment for uneasiness, and there are a few strategies that can be utilized to assist with overseeing side effects. These methods incorporate mental rebuilding, openness treatment, unwinding procedures, and care. Contextual investigations and models can assist with showing how these procedures can be applied to tension and can give trust and motivation to the individuals who are battling with this condition.

Chapter 6:

Applying CBT to Insomnia

Understanding Insomnia

A sleeping disorder is a typical rest problem portrayed by trouble nodding off, staying unconscious, or getting up too soon and not having the option to fall back snoozing. It can essentially affect an individual's satisfaction and work, and it is critical to look for treatment if you are encountering side effects of sleep deprivation.

CBT Techniques for Insomnia

CBT is a viable treatment for a sleeping disorder, and there are a few methods that can be utilized to assist with overseeing side effects. A portion of these methods include:

- **Rest Cleanliness:** Laying out a normal rest plan, making a loosening up sleep schedule, and trying not to invigorate exercises before sleep time.

- **Improvement Control:** Connecting the bed and room with rest by utilizing the bed just for rest and sex, and keeping away from exercises like sitting in front of the television or involving electronic gadgets in bed.
- **Rest Limitation:** Restricting how much time is spent in bed to increment rest effectiveness and combine rest.
- **Unwinding Procedures:** Learning and rehearsing unwinding methods like profound breathing, moderate muscle unwinding, and directed symbolism to diminish pressure and tension.
- **Mental Rebuilding:** Distinguishing and testing negative idea examples and supplanting them with additional versatile and reasonable considerations about rest.

In outline, CBT is a compelling treatment for sleep deprivation, and there are a few procedures that can be utilized to assist with overseeing side effects. These procedures incorporate rest cleanliness, boost control, rest limitation, unwinding strategies, and mental rebuilding. It means quite a bit to work with a certified specialist or rest expert to foster a customized treatment plan that tends to your particular necessities and concerns.

Chapter 7:

Applying CBT to Intrusive Thought

Understanding Intrusive Thoughts

Meddling considerations are undesirable and upsetting contemplations, pictures, or urges that over and over occur to an individual. They can be upsetting and cause huge pain and nervousness. Meddlesome considerations are a typical encounter and are not an indication of an emotional wellness problem. In any case, assuming that they are causing critical trouble or disrupting everyday work, looking for treatment might be useful.

CBT Procedures for Intrusive Thoughts

CBT is a successful treatment for meddling considerations, and there are a few procedures that can be utilized to assist with overseeing side effects. A portion of these strategies includes:

- **Mental Rebuilding:** Distinguishing and testing negative idea examples and supplanting them with additional versatile and sensible considerations.

-   **Openness and Reaction Anticipation (ERP):** Slowly presenting the client with dreaded contemplations or circumstances and forestalling the typical reaction (e.g., aversion or impulses) to decrease uneasiness and trouble.

- **Care:** Rehearsing care methods, for example, contemplation and care-based pressure decrease to expand mindfulness and acknowledgment of considerations and feelings.

- **Acknowledgment and Responsibility Treatment (ACT):** Figuring out how to acknowledge and endure upsetting contemplations and feelings, and resolving to values-based activities.

In synopsis, CBT is a powerful treatment for nosy contemplations, and there are a few methods that can be utilized to assist with overseeing side effects. These strategies incorporate mental rebuilding, openness and reaction counteraction, care, and acknowledgment and responsibility treatment. It means quite a bit to work with a certified specialist to foster a customized treatment plan that tends to your particular necessities and concerns.

Chapter 8:

Applying CBT to Anger

Understanding Anger

Anger is a normal and natural emotion that everyone experiences from time to time. However, when anger becomes excessive or uncontrollable, it can hurt a person's relationships, health, and overall well-being. It is important to understand the underlying causes of anger and to develop healthy ways of managing and expressing it.

CBT Techniques for Anger

CBT is an effective treatment for anger, and several techniques can be used to help manage symptoms. Some of these techniques include:

- **Cognitive Restructuring:** Identifying and challenging negative thought patterns and replacing them with more adaptive and realistic thoughts.

- **Anger Management Skills:** Learning and practicing skills such as deep breathing, progressive muscle relaxation, and assertive communication to reduce stress and anxiety.
- **Problem-solving:** Developing effective problem-solving skills to address the underlying causes of anger and find constructive solutions.
- **BehavioralActivation:** Increasing engagement in positive and rewarding activities to improve mood and reduce symptoms of anger.
- **Relaxation Techniques:** Learning and practicing relaxation techniques such as deep breathing, progressive muscle relaxation, and guided imagery to reduce stress and anxiety.

In summary, CBT is an effective treatment for anger, and several techniques can be used to help manage symptoms. These techniques include cognitive restructuring, anger management skills, problem-solving, behavioral activation, and relaxation techniques. It is important to work with a qualified therapist to develop a personalized treatment plan that addresses your specific needs and concerns.

Chapter 9:

CBT for Special Populations

CBT for Youngsters and Adolescents

CBT can be a powerful treatment for kids and teenagers who are encountering an extensive variety of psychological well-being issues, including sadness, tension, ADHD, and conduct issues. CBT for youngsters and teenagers is ordinarily adjusted to be fitting and may include the utilization of games, exercises, and inventive procedures to connect with more youthful clients. A few normal strategies utilized in CBT for kids and teenagers include:

- **Play Treatment:** Utilizing play to assist youngsters with offering their viewpoints and sentiments and to rehearse new abilities and procedures.
- **Conduct Parent Preparing:** Helping guardians with viable nurturing abilities

and systems to deal with their youngster's way of behaving.

- **Interactive abilities Preparing:** Showing youngsters and youths interactive abilities, for example, correspondence, critical thinking, and compromise.

CBT for Older Adults

CBT can likewise be a powerful treatment for more established grown-ups who are encountering psychological wellness issues like discouragement, tension, and mental deterioration. CBT for more seasoned grown-ups may zero in on tending to the special difficulties and stressors that more established grown-ups face, for example, persistent medical issues, loss of freedom, and social disengagement. A few normal strategies utilized in CBT for more established grown-ups include:

- **Critical thinking:** Assisting more established grown-ups with creating viable critical thinking abilities to address life stressors and difficulties.

- **Social Actuation:** Expanding commitment in sure and remunerating exercises to further develop mindset and diminish side effects of sorrow.
- **Mental Rebuilding:** Recognizing and testing negative idea examples and supplanting them with additional versatile and sensible considerations.

CBT for Couples and Families

CBT can likewise be a powerful treatment for couples and families who are encountering relationship issues, correspondence issues, and struggles. CBT for couples and families might zero in on further developing correspondence, settling clashes, and creating compelling critical thinking abilities. A few normal strategies utilized in CBT for couples and families include:

- **Relational abilities Preparing:** Showing couples and families powerful relational abilities like undivided attention, confident correspondence, and compromise.

- **Critical thinking:** Assisting couples and families with creating compelling critical thinking abilities to address relationship issues and clashes.
- **ConductEnactment:** Expanding commitment in certain and remunerating exercises to further develop temperament and decrease side effects of sadness.

In rundown, CBT can be a successful treatment for an extensive variety of psychological well-being issues in exceptional populations like youngsters and youths, more established grown-ups, and couples and families. It is vital to work with a certified specialist who has experience working with these populations to foster a customized treatment plan that tends to their particular requirements and concerns.

Chapter 10:

Integrating CBT with Other Therapies

CBT and Medication

CBT can be utilized related to medicine to treat an extensive variety of psychological well-being issues, including despondency, uneasiness, and bipolar problems. CBT and medicine can be correlative medicines, and exploration has demonstrated the way that consolidating the two can prompt improved results than either treatment alone. A few well-known ways that CBT and drugs can be coordinated include:

- **Psychoeducation:** Giving data to clients about the advantages and expected results of medicine and assisting them with settling on informed conclusions about their treatment.
- **Checking:** Observing clients' side effects and progress over the long haul to decide whether drug changes are required.

- **Joint effort:** Working cooperatively with clients endorsing doctors to organize care and guarantee that treatment is successful and proper.

CBT and Mindfulness

CBT and care are two helpful methodologies that can be utilized together to treat an extensive variety of emotional well-being issues, including discouragement, nervousness, and stress. Care is the act of focusing on the current second with receptiveness, interest, and acknowledgment. A few familiar ways that CBT and care can be coordinated include:

- **Care Based Mental Treatment (MBCT):** Consolidating care procedures with mental rebuilding to assist clients with growing more versatile and sensible contemplations.
- **Care Based Pressure Decrease (MBSR):** Utilizing care strategies to diminish

pressure and uneasiness and work on by and large prosperity.

- **Care Activities:** Showing clients care activities like contemplation, profound breathing, and body checking to assist them with creating more prominent mindfulness and acknowledgment of their viewpoints and feelings.

CBT and Acceptance and Commitment Therapy (ACT)

CBT and Acknowledgment and Responsibility Treatment (ACT) are two helpful methodologies that can be utilized together to treat an extensive variety of emotional well-being issues, including discouragement, nervousness, and injury. ACT depends on the possibility that mental enduring is made by the battle control or keeping away from undesirable contemplations and feelings, and that acknowledgment and care can assist clients with creating more noteworthy mental adaptability and strength. A few familiar ways that CBT and ACT can be coordinated include:

- **Mental Defusion:** Utilizing mental defusion methods to assist clients with creating more prominent separation from their viewpoints and feelings and decrease their effect.
- **Values Explanation:** Assisting clients with explaining their qualities and objectives and fostering a feeling of direction and importance.
- **Serious Activity:** Empower clients to make a move by their qualities and objectives, even notwithstanding troublesome considerations and feelings.

In rundown, CBT can be coordinated with other restorative methodologies like drug, care, and ACT to treat an extensive variety of emotional well-being issues. It is critical to work with a certified specialist who has insight into these ways to deal with foster a customized treatment plan that tends to your particular necessities and concerns

Chapter 11:

Self-Help Strategies and Resources

Self-improvement Guides and Workbooks

Self-improvement guides and exercise manuals are assets that people can use to address various private matters and difficulties. These assets normally give data, systems, and activities to help perusers comprehend and defeat their challenges. Some well-known self-improvement guides and exercise manuals cover subjects, for example, nervousness, melancholy, stress the executives, relationship issues, and self-awareness.

Online Resources and Apps

The web offers an abundance of assets for self-improvement and self-awareness. Online assets can incorporate articles, recordings, digital broadcasts, and intelligent devices that give data and direction on a great many themes.

Furthermore, there are numerous versatile applications accessible that offer self-improvement devices, for example, contemplation and care applications, mindset following applications, and applications for overseeing nervousness and stress.

Support Groups and Peer Support

Support gatherings and friend-encouraging groups of people can be significant assets for people looking for help and backing. These gatherings give a protected and strong climate where people can share their encounters, get support and guidance, and interface with other people who are confronting comparative difficulties. Support gatherings can be found face-to-face, on the web, or through virtual entertainment stages.

By and large, self-improvement procedures and assets can be significant apparatuses for people looking to work on their psychological well-being and prosperity. Whether through self-improvement guides, online assets, or care groups, there are numerous choices accessible for people hoping to assume command over their emotional well-being and roll out certain improvements in their lives.

Conclusion

All in all, "The Ultimate Guide to CBT: Transform Your Life with Proven Strategies for Overcoming Depression, Anxiety, Insomnia, Intrusive Thoughts, and Anger" gives an exhaustive and down-to-earth way to deal with Cognitive Behavioral Treatment (CBT). By understanding the standards and methods of CBT, perusers can figure out how to recognize and challenge pessimistic idea designs, deal with feelings, and foster better survival techniques. This book enables people to assume command over their psychological wellness and change their lives to improve things. Whether you are battling with discouragement, tension, sleep deprivation, meddling considerations, or outrage, CBT offers a way to mend and develop. With commitment and practice, you can conquer your difficulties and carry on with a seriously satisfying and healthy lifestyle.